L'ANGLAIS POUR LES ENFANTS

READ ENGLISH WITH ZIGZAG -1

ISBN: 978-1-914911-08-8

www.zigzagenglish.co.uk

www.zigzagenglish.co.uk – BOOKS FOR ENGLISH LEARNERS

OUR BOOKS FOR CHILDREN

Our bilingual picture books for younger children. *Funny stories in simple, useful everyday English, with colour photos.*
English with Tony -1- Tony moves house
English with Tony -2- Tony is happy
English with Tony -3- Tony's Christmas
English with Tony -4- Tony's holiday
My best friend

Our coursebook for beginners *(age 7 to 11)*
English for Children - 1st Coursebook *(Essential vocabulary and grammar for beginners)*

Our dialogue books for beginners *(age 7 to 11).*
I Speak English Too! - 1
I Speak English Too! - 2

Our series of reading and comprehension books for beginners *(age 7 to 11).*
Read English with Zigzag - 1
Read English with Zigzag - 2
Read English with Zigzag - 3
Audiobook at Audible.com

Our vocabulary book with photos, word puzzles and more *(age 7+)*
300+ mots en anglais / 300+ englische Wörter / 300+ palabras en inglés / 300+ parole inglesi

The Learn English Activity Book for Children *(A1 - A2, elementary). (Recommended for children in early secondary school.)*

Our series of reading and comprehension books for children at elementary level *(A1 - A2) (recommended for ages 10 to 13). With lots of language activities.*
Read English with Ben - 1
Read English with Ben - 2
Read English with Ben - 3

Our YOU DECIDE adventure book with 1 beginning and 19 endings. *A2 (11+)* Your Bilingual Fairy Tale Adventure

Our series of reading and discussion books about a family with superpowers *(with writing tasks) for children at secondary school, A2 - B1*
I Live in a Castle – Book 1 – My Superpower
I Live in a Castle – Book 2 – The New Me

The Speak English, Read English, Write English Activity Books – *3 books from A1 to B2, for older children and adults.*

Our non-fiction book with language activities
Learn English with Fun Facts! – A2 - B2

English Dialogues for Teenagers – for ages 11 to 17, A2 - B2

OUR BOOKS FOR ADULTS

Our 3 Grammar books with grammar-focused dialogues
Learn English Grammar through Conversation – A1, A2 and B1

Our Dialogue books for adults *(with vocabulary lists and comprehension questions). Audiobooks are available for some of these books – at Audible.com.*
50 very Easy Everyday English Dialogues (A2)
50 Easy Everyday English Dialogues (A2 - B1)
50 Intermediate Everyday English Dialogues (B1 - B2)
50 more Intermediate Everyday English Dialogues (B1 - B2)
40 Advanced Everyday English Dialogues (B2 - C1)
40 Intermediate Business English Dialogues (B1 - B2)
40 Advanced Business English Dialogues (B2 - C1)

Our activity books for adults and older children
The Speak English, Read English, Write English Activity Books – 3 books, for A1 - A2, A2 - B1 and B1 - B2.

Our non-fiction book with language activities
Learn English with Fun Facts! – A2 - B2

Contents

Les objectifs de cette série de livres:

1. Proposer une lecture amusante et drôle.
2. Donner à votre enfant la confiance nécessaire pour lire en anglais.
3. Enseigner à votre enfant des mots et des phrases clés. Les livres les présentent, les répètent et les développent petit à petit, afin d'élargir la compréhension de votre enfant.
4. Aider votre enfant à apprendre la grammaire anglaise essentielle de manière ludique.

Comment utiliser cette série de livres:

1. Votre enfant pourra peut-être h lire les livres tout seul. C'est très bien! Mais si vous parlez anglais, vous pouvez l'aider à améliorer sa prononciation en l'encourageant à lire à haute voix. **Les livres 1 et 2 sont également disponibles en livre audio**.
2. Il y a des listes de vocabulaire, pour aider votre enfant à comprendre le texte et à apprendre de nouveaux mots.
3. Il y a des questions de compréhension, dont les réponses se trouvent à la fin de chaque livre.
4. Il y a des activités linguistiques pour aider votre enfant à enrichir son vocabulaire et sa grammaire.

Quoi d'autre? Et après?

1. Notre série de dialogues simples - **I Speak English Too!** - est conçue pour les parents qui souhaitent aider leur enfant à commencer à parler anglais. Elle est idéale pour 1 parent et 1 enfant, ou pour 2 enfants. Elle commence par les bases, en présentant et en développant des mots et des phrases clés pour aider votre enfant à faire des progrès rapides. En quelques leçons, votre enfant pourra avoir de petites conversations en anglais avec vous.
2. Lire des livres (très simples) en anglais fait une grande différence. Nous vous recommandons également de regarder des séries télévisées simples pour enfants, même si elles sont conçues pour les enfants de langue maternelle anglaise qui sont un peu plus jeunes que votre enfant. Les livres audio sont également excellents, surtout juste avant d'aller se coucher (ce qui aide l'enfant à retenir la nouvelle langue). Ne vous attendez pas à ce que votre enfant comprenne tout tout de suite - les livres audio peuvent être écoutés à plusieurs reprises, et votre enfant comprendra mieux à chaque fois.

Early morning at Zigzag's house

1 I'm Zigzag

Hello! My name's Zigzag. Yes, Zigzag. My name's Zigzag.

I'm six. And I'm a **tiger**. I'm not a cat. No, I'm not a big cat. I'm a tiger. I'm a small tiger.

What's your name? Are you a tiger? No? Are you a boy? Are you a girl? Are you big or small?

How old are you? Are you eight or nine? Or ten or eleven? I'm six.

I like big boys and girls. And I like small girls and boys.

I like **chicken** and **cheese**. And I like **cat food**. But I'm not a cat. No, I'm not. I'm a tiger.

I'm **busy today**. I'm very busy. I'm very, very busy. Are you busy?

I have to go now, because I'm busy. Can I see you **tomorrow**? Please? Please, please, please, please, please? Yes? Thank you!

Goodbye! See you tomorrow!

Vocabulary

• tiger	tigre
• chicken	poulet
• cheese	fromage
• cat food	nourriture pour chats
• busy	occupé
• today	aujourd'hui
• tomorrow	demain

2 Poppy

Poppy is eight. She **lives** in a nice house in Cambridge. Cambridge is a small **city** in **England**.

Poppy lives with her mum and dad. She has a **little** brother. His name is Adam. He's four. She doesn't have any sisters. But she has two pets - a dog and a cat.

Her cat is called Zigzag. He's **really** big. He **looks like** a little tiger. Her dog is called Pam. She's **quite** big too. She's black and white.

Poppy likes playing with her cat and her dog. And she likes playing with her friends, **too**.

Questions:

1. *Where does Poppy live?*
2. *How old is Adam?*
3. *How many pets does Poppy have?*

Vocabulary

- to live — vivre
- city — ville
- England — Angleterre
- little — petit
- really — vraiment
- to look like — ressembler à
- quite — assez
- too — aussi

3 How many animals do you know?

Where is the: hamster, butterfly, spider, rabbit, snail, fish, rat, bird and snake?

4 Pam's a dog

Hello! Hello everyone! I'm Zigzag. My name's Zigzag. What's your name? Is your name Anne? No? Is it Mark? No? What IS your name? How old are you? I'm six!

This is my friend. This is my friend Pam. Pam is a dog. I'm a tiger, **but** Pam's a dog. I'm a small tiger, and Pam is a big dog. I AM NOT A CAT!

I like Pam. I don't like dogs, but I like Pam. Pam is a good dog.

Do you like dogs? Do you like dogs and tigers? Or do you like snakes and spiders?

I'm very **hungry**. I want to **eat** cat food. Pam is hungry too. Pam wants to eat dog food. Cat food is **nice**, but dog food is horrible. **Yuck**!

Vocabulary

- but mais
- I'm hungry j'ai faim
- to eat manger
- nice bon
- yuck beurk

5 Do you have a pet?

Do you have a hamster or a rabbit? A fish or a bird? A rat or a snake?

Or do you have a cat or a dog? Which is **better**? You **choose**!

CAT or DOG?

Easy to look after?

Friendly?

Intelligent?

Fun?

Funny?

Independent?

Cute?

Beautiful?

Vocabulary

• pet	animal de compagnie
• better	meilleur
• to choose	choisir
• easy	facile
• to look after	s'occuper de
• friendly	amical
• fun	amusant
• funny	drôle
• cute	mignon
• beautiful	beau

6 It's my sofa

Hello! How are you? How are you today? Are you okay? I'm fine. Pam's fine too.

This is my house. My house is big. My house is **lovely**. Do you like my house?

This is my sofa. My **sofa** is very **comfortable**. I like my sofa. Pam likes my sofa too. But it's MY sofa! Go away, Pam!

This is my **kitchen**. This is my **fridge**. This is my cat food in the fridge.

I'm hungry. I want my cat food!

This is Poppy. Poppy, **give** me my cat food! Please, Poppy!

Thank you!

Vocabulary

- lovely — beau, très bien
- sofa — canapé
- comfortable — confortable
- kitchen — cuisine
- fridge — réfrigérateur
- to give — donner

7 Adam's hungry

Adam's hungry. He wants to eat:

Ice cream, crisps, biscuits, a doughnut, chocolate and sweets.

His mum wants him to eat:

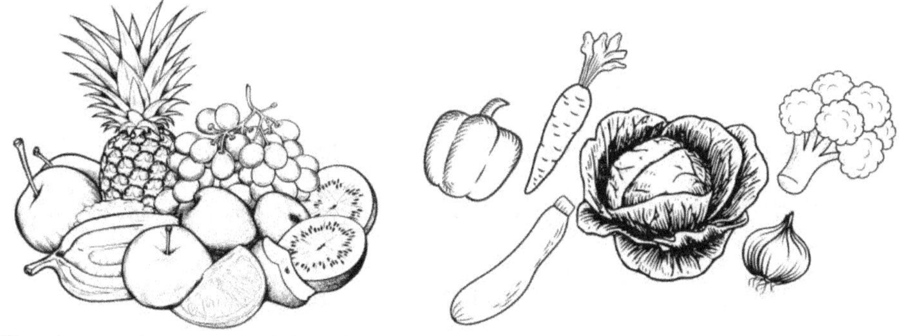

Fruit and vegetables!

Are you hungry? What do *you* want to eat?

8 I don't want to eat cat food

Hello! How are you? I'm okay today. I'm fine.

But I'm hungry. I want to eat **something**. I don't want to eat cat food. And I don't want to eat dog food. Dog food is horrible -yuck!

I want to eat... a spider! I like spiders. I like eating spiders. I like eating big, black spiders! Do you like eating spiders?

Is there a spider in the fridge? No, there's not. Is there a spider in the **garden**? Let's **look for** a spider.

Is this a spider? No, it's not a spider. It's a snail. It's a small snail. What colour is it? It's brown and white. I don't like snails.

Is this a spider? No, it's not. It's a butterfly. It's a beautiful butterfly. What colour is it? It's red, yellow and blue. I like butterflies. Butterflies are nice. They're **pretty**. But I don't like eating butterflies.

I want to eat a spider!

Vocabulary

• something	quelque chose
• garden	jardin
• to look for	chercher
• pretty	joli

9 Poppy goes to school

Poppy goes to school **every day**. No, not every day. Poppy goes to school on Monday, Tuesday, Wednesday, Thursday and Friday.

Adam doesn't go to school. He's too small to go to school. But he goes to **nursery**. Poppy likes going to school, but Adam doesn't like going to nursery. He wants to **stay** at home. He wants to play with the dog in the garden.

Poppy doesn't go to school on Saturday or Sunday. At the weekend, Poppy stays at home and plays with her little brother. Sometimes she goes to the park. Sometimes she goes to a friend's house.

Poppy has a **best friend**. She's called Jessica. Jessica is a beautiful name!

Questions:

1. *Does Adam go to school?*
2. *When doesn't Poppy go to school?*
3. *Where does Poppy go at the weekend?*

Vocabulary

- every day — tous les jours
- nursery — crèche
- to stay — rester
- best friend — meilleur ami

10 Where's my toy?

Hi! Is that you? Is that you **again**? It's nice to see you!

I **feel great**. I'm not hungry. I'm not hungry now. I don't want any cat food. I don't want **another** spider. One spider is **enough**.

Where is my **toy**? I want to play with it.

Is it **on** the table? No, it's not.

Is it **under** the sofa? No, it's not.

Is it **behind** the **armchair**? No, it's not.

Where is it? Oh, there it is. It's **next to** the television.

Pam, do you want to play with me? No, she doesn't want to play.

Poppy, do you want to play with me? No, she doesn't.

Adam, do you want to play? Adam? Where are you?

Yes! Yes! Adam wants to play. He wants to play with me! I love you, Adam!

Vocabulary

- again encore
- to feel se sentir
- great très bien.
- another un autre
- enough assez
- toy jouet
- on sur
- under sous
- behind derrière
- armchair fauteuil
- next to à côté de

11 School

Poppy and Jessica **walk** to school with Jessica's mum.

Their school is quite big. There are three hundred and fifty children at the school. There are twenty-five children in Poppy's class and twenty-six children in Jessica's class. Jessica's class is bigger than Poppy's.

Poppy's teacher is called Mrs Rice. She's nice. Poppy likes her - most of the time!

Poppy likes **learning** English, but she doesn't like maths. Maths is fun, but Poppy doesn't like it. She's bad at maths, but she's very good at English. Poppy likes **break times** best. Sometimes Poppy and her friends play football. Sometimes they **chat**.

On Thursdays, Poppy takes her **swimming things** to school. All the children in her class go swimming at the big **swimming pool** near their school. Everyone loves swimming. Thursday is the **best** day of the week.

Questions:

1. *Does Poppy go to school **by car**?*

2. *How big is Poppy's school?*
3. *Does Poppy like maths lessons best?*

Vocabulary

- to walk — aller à pied
- to learn — apprendre
- break time — pause
- to chat — discuter
- swimming things — maillot de bain et serviette
- swimming pool — piscine
- best — meilleur
- by car — en voiture

12 It's not my fault

Oh dear. **I'm sorry**. I'm really sorry, Adam.

Does it hurt, Adam?

I'm sorry. But **it's not my fault**. It's really not my fault, is it Adam? It's your fault, isn't it Adam?

Adam is **sad**. Adam has to go to the **doctor's**.

But I want to play. Where's my toy now? Poppy? Do you want to play with me?

Please play with me Poppy! Why not? Why are you **angry**? Why are you angry with me?

I'm sad now. I'm **tired**. I'm hungry. I'm really hungry. I want my cat food!

Vocabulary

- sorry — désolé
- to hurt — faire mal
- it's not my fault — ce n'est pas ma faute
- sad — triste
- doctor — médecin
- angry — en colère
- tired — fatigué

13 At the doctor's

Adam has to go to the doctor's today. Poppy goes with him.

The doctor looks at Adam's **hand**. His **left** hand. There's a **scratch** on his hand.

"Is there a cat at home?" asks the doctor.

"Yes", says Adam. "I like the cat, but he doesn't like me!"

The doctor puts a **plaster** on Adam's hand. "It's not a bad scratch," he says. "But **be careful** when you play with that cat. Maybe it's really a tiger?"

Questions:

1. ***Who** goes to the doctor's with Adam?*
2. *Is there a scratch on Adam's **right** hand?*
3. *What does the doctor put on Adam's hand?*

Vocabulary

• hand	main
• left	gauche
• scratch	éraflure
• plaster	sparadrap
• be careful	fais attention
• who	qui
• right	droit

14 I'm sorry

Hello! How are you? Are you okay?

I'm fine. But Adam's not fine. **Poor** Adam.

Look at Adam's hand. He has a big plaster on his hand. Does your hand hurt, Adam?

His left hand hurts, but his right hand doesn't hurt. His right hand is okay.

Adam, can you play with me? Can you play with me with your right hand? Can you?

He doesn't want to play.

Adam, this is for you. This is a **present** for you.

It's a lovely big black spider.

Because I love you, Adam. And because I'm really sorry.

Vocabulary

- poor pauvre
- present cadeau

15 Birthday party

Poppy wants to **invite** everyone in her class to her **birthday party**. But her mum says no. Poppy can invite nine friends.

Poppy **chooses** Jessica and eight other friends. Choosing's not easy.

Poppy's birthday party is so much fun. She gets lots of presents. The best present is a toy dog that **barks.** It looks just like Pam.

The chocolate cake is enormous. Chocolate cake is Poppy's favourite.

Everyone sings Happy Birthday. **Some** of the children are very bad **singers**!

The party **games** are great. The best game is Musical **Chairs**. When the **music stops**, you have to **sit** on a chair. But there aren't enough chairs! Jessica **wins** that game.

Then there are **races** in the garden. Adam wins the **egg** and **spoon** race.

Questions:

1. *How big is the birthday cake?*
2. *What do the children have to do when the music stops?*

Vocabulary

- to invite — inviter
- birthday party — fête d'anniversaire
- to choose — choisir
- to bark — aboyer
- everyone — tout le monde
- some — certains
- singer — chanteur
- game — jeu
- chair — chaise
- music — musique
- to stop — s'arrêter
- to sit — s'asseoir
- to win — gagner
- race — course
- egg — œuf
- spoon — cuillère

H A P P Y B I

16 Too many boys and girls

Hi there! Is it your birthday today?

It's Poppy's birthday today. Poppy is nine today.

I don't like birthday parties. They're **noisy**. They're too noisy. There are lots of children. There are too many children.

Pam likes birthday parties. She likes noisy children. She likes eating birthday cake too.

I can't sit on my sofa. There are too many children in the living room! I can't eat my cat food. There are too many children in the kitchen! I can't look for a spider in the garden. **That's right** -there are too many boys and girls there!

Mum and Dad's bedroom is **quiet**. Their bed is quite comfortable.

See you tomorrow...

Vocabulary

- noisy — bruyant
- that's right — c'est ça
- quiet — calme, tranquille

17 Party games

This is Poppy's favourite party game. It's called Musical Statues.

Play some music. Everyone **dances**.

When the music stops, everyone has to **stand still. Completely** still.

If you **move**, you're out of the game.

Play the music again.

The winner is the **last** person **left**.

Adam's favourite race is the egg and spoon race.

Everyone gets a spoon and an egg.

You have to put the egg in the spoon and run with it.

If you **drop** the egg, you have to **pick it up** and put it back in the spoon.

If you use **real** eggs, this race can get very **messy**!

Vocabulary

- to dance — danser
- to stand still — rester immobile
- completely — complètement
- to move — bouger
- last — dernier

- left — qui reste
- to drop — laisser tomber
- to pick up — ramasser
- real — vrai
- messy — salissant

18 A very small house

Look at this. It's a house. But it's very, very small.

I don't **understand**. Do you understand?

Who lives in this house? Very, very small **people**?

Where are the small people?

Are they **hiding**? Are they hiding in the yellow toy **box**? Are they hiding under the purple armchair? Are they hiding behind the white **bookcase**?

Is there a very small dog too? And a very small tiger?

I don't understand!

Vocabulary

understand	comprendre
people	personnes, gens
to hide	cacher
box	boîte
bookcase	bibliothèque

19 A weekend at the seaside

It's **summer** now. It's hot. It's too hot.

Poppy's **excited**. The family is **going away** for the weekend. They're going to a hotel by the **sea**.

Poppy packs her swimming things - her green **swimming costume** and her **towel**. Adam packs his red **plastic bucket**.

Pam is going to the seaside too. She's very **happy**. She takes her **ball**.

Adam puts Zigzag's cat toy in the car.

"Zigzag is a cat!" says Mum. "He can't come!"

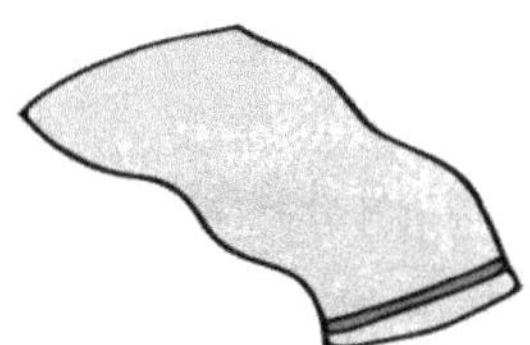

Questions:

1. *Is Poppy going to the mountains?*
2. *What does Pam take with her?*
3. *Why can't Zigzag come?*

Vocabulary

- seaside bord de la mer
- summer l'été
- excited excité
- to go away partir
- sea mer
- swimming costume maillot de bain
- towel serviette
- plastic plastique
- bucket seau
- happy heureux
- ball balle, ballon

20 The Boss

Hello. Is that you again? I want to tell you a secret.

Today is an important day.

Today, Mum and Dad and Poppy and Adam and Pam aren't here.

Tomorrow's an important day too. Because tomorrow, Pam and Adam and Poppy and Dad and Mum aren't here.

But I'm here. I'm in the house. Today and tomorrow, this is MY house. I AM THE BOSS.

And this is what I want to do...

Vocabulary

- boss patron

21 Where are they?

in front of? in?

between? next to?

behind? on?

under?

22 I want to…

I want to:

Eat all the cat food.

Chase birds in the garden.

Scratch Dad's **special** chair.

Lick the little people in the **doll's house**.

Run up and down the **stairs** ten times.

Pull the children's **pictures off** the fridge.

Bite the **next door neighbour**.

Drink water from the toilet.

Go to sleep in Mum and Dad's bed.

PURRRRRRR… That was so much fun.

Vocabulary

• to chase	chasser
• special	spécial
• to lick	lécher
• doll’s house	maison de poupée
• stairs	escalier
• to pull off	arracher
• picture	dessin, peinture
• to bite	mordre
• next door neighbour	voisin d'à côté
• to drink	boire
• toilet	toilette
• to go to sleep	s’endormir

Word Search

Z	U	O	I	H	X	V	F	P	X	I	L	D	N	H
Y	D	H	Y	C	E	N	I	U	E	B	H	W	E	G
Z	U	N	D	E	R	S	T	A	N	D	A	W	I	A
G	A	M	E	N	F	B	G	Q	K	S	E	Z	G	R
F	J	F	U	I	A	T	L	D	A	L	N	P	H	D
C	L	P	B	C	H	O	C	O	L	A	T	E	B	E
X	Q	Z	K	G	Z	M	F	S	A	V	E	O	O	N
S	T	A	I	R	S	O	R	O	S	K	C	P	U	K
X	R	N	L	C	Z	R	I	F	W	U	I	L	R	O
M	D	Q	D	V	O	R	D	A	M	U	B	E	Q	Z
J	Z	K	H	Y	Z	O	G	E	O	A	B	X	X	A
G	J	Y	C	Z	M	W	E	S	H	P	C	N	G	Q
V	F	G	R	Y	S	I	M	L	N	R	C	D	E	Z
S	F	H	M	O	E	F	Q	X	L	Q	K	U	O	X
S	U	W	X	B	A	L	O	V	E	L	Y	H	D	Z

- It's summer. It's hot. I want to swim in the **s-a**.
- My **n-ighb-ur** has a **l-v-ly g-rd-n**.
- Why is the in the **fr-d-e**? Because it's hot today.
- Zigzag runs up and down the **st-ir-** all day.
- I don't **und-rst-nd** how to play the **ga-e** of Musical Chairs.
- There are 2 **peo-le** on my **s-f-**! Get off, it's MY **s-f-**!
- What do you want to do **t-m-rr-w**, Zigzag? I want to eat all the cat food!

Réponses:

2

1. She lives in Cambridge in England.
2. He's four.
3. She has two pets.

3

snail, butterfly, fish, rat, spider, snake, hamster, bird, rabbit

9

1. No, he doesn't. He goes to nursery.
2. At the weekend (on Saturday and Sunday).
3. She goes to the park or to a friend's house.

11

1. No, she doesn't. She walks to school.
2. It's quite big.
3. No, she doesn't. She likes break times best.

13

1. Poppy does. Poppy goes with him.
2. No, there's not. There's a scratch on his left hand.
3. The doctor puts a plaster on Adam's hand.

15

1. It's enormous.
2. They have to sit on a chair.

19

1. No, she's not. She's going to the seaside.
2. She takes her ball with her.
3. Because he's a cat.

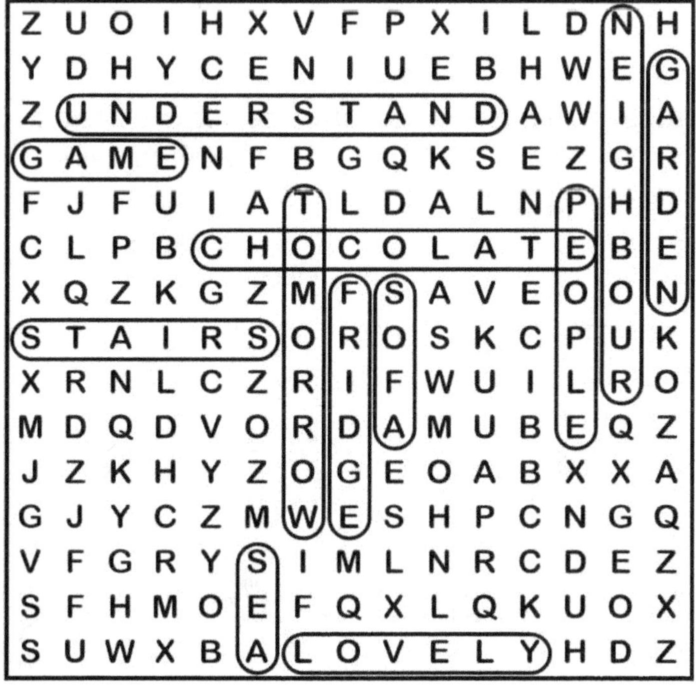

Merci d'avoir lu ce livre!

Si vous avez des questions ou des suggestions pour améliorer le livre, vous pouvez m'envoyer un courriel à l'adresse suivante: lydiawinter.zigzagenglish@gmail.com.
Les suggestions pour de nouveaux livres sont toujours les bienvenues.

Vous trouverez le site web de Zigzag English ici:
www.zigzagenglish.co.uk.
Votre enfant et vous pouvez découvrir nos autres livres pour enfants et adultes, lire le blog et faire d'autres activités en anglais.

N'hésitez pas à laisser un avis pour ce livre. Merci beaucoup!

Dans les pages suivantes, vous trouverez des extraits d'autres livres destinés aux enfants de niveau débutant à élémentaire.

From: ***Read English with Zigzag - 2***

5 Where is Poppy?

Hi there!

Can I **ask you a question**?

Where is Poppy? Why isn't she here? Where does she go every day?

Is she hiding in the house?

Is she outside, in the garden?

Do you know where she is?

I'm looking for Poppy. I'm looking for her **downstairs**, in the living-room and the kitchen. And I'm looking for her upstairs, in the bedrooms and the bathroom.

I'm looking for her **inside**, and I'm looking for her outside.

But I can't find her. Why not? Please **help** me find her!

From: ***I Speak English Too! – 1***

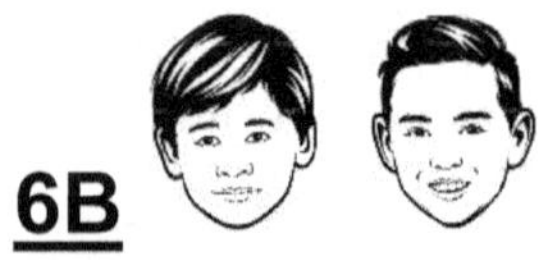

6B

Jack: I really want a dog, Sam.

Sam: Don't you have a cat?

Jack: Yes, I do. I like my cat, but I want a dog too.

Sam: Dogs are nice, but they're very **messy**.

Jack: Cats aren't messy. But they're a bit boring.

Sam: Cats are beautiful. I want a cat, but my dad doesn't want one.

Jack: Does your mum want a cat?

Sam: Yes, she does. She likes cats a lot. But my dad really doesn't like them.

Jack: Does your brother like cats **or** dogs?

Sam: He likes **snakes**.

Jack: Snakes? I **hate** snakes!

From: ***The Learn English Activity Book for Children***

CHOOSE!

You can't always have everything you want.
Sometimes you have to choose.
So what do you choose?

- Ice cream or chocolate?
- A hamster or a rabbit?
- Homework or **housework**?
- A holiday at the beach or a skiing holiday?
- One very good friend or three good friends?
- Football or swimming?
- A green bedroom or a white bedroom?
- Autumn or spring?
- Chinese food or Italian food?
- Very hot **weather** or very cold weather?
- Orange juice or a milkshake?

www.ingramcontent.com/pod-product-compliance
Lightning Source LLC
LaVergne TN
LVHW010108110826
845155LV00028B/544

9781914911088